Paid for by donations

from the

Mount Laurel Community

NATURE'S LIGHT SHOW

RAINBOWS

By Kristen Rajczak

Gareth Stevens
Publishing

Please visit our website, www.garethstevens.com. For a free color catalog of all our high-quality books, call toll free 1-800-542-2595 or fax 1-877-542-2596.

Library of Congress Cataloging-in-Publication Data

Rajczak, Kristen.
Rainbows / Kristen Rajczak.
    p. cm. — (Nature's light show)
Includes index.
ISBN 978-1-4339-7032-0 (pbk.)
ISBN 978-1-4339-7033-7 (6-pack)
ISBN 978-1-4339-7031-3 (library binding)
1. Rainbows—Juvenile literature. 2. Light—Juvenile literature. I. Title.
QC976.R2R36 2013
551.56'7—dc23

2011045160

First Edition

Published in 2013 by
Gareth Stevens Publishing
111 East 14th Street, Suite 349
New York, NY 10003

Designer: Katelyn E. Reynolds
Editor: Kristen Rajczak

Photo credits: Cover, pp. 1, 4, 5, 9, 21 (main), (cover, pp. 1, 3–24 background) Shutterstock.com; p. 6 Brand X Pictures/Thinkstock; p. 7 Dimitri Vervitsiotis/Photographer's Choice RF/Getty Images; p. 12 Hemera/Thinkstock; p. 13 Last Refuge/Robert Harding World Imagery/Getty Images; p. 15 Adam Jones/The Image Bank/Getty Images; p. 16 Claidheamdanns/Wikipedia; p. 17 courtesy Calvin Bradshaw (calvinbradshaw.com); pp. 18, 20 iStockphoto/Thinkstock; p. 19 R. Tyler Gross/Getty Images; p. 21 (inset) Dorling Kindersley/Getty Images.

Printed in the United States of America

CPSIA compliance information: Batch #CS12GS: For further information contact Gareth Stevens, New York, New York at 1-800-542-2595.

CONTENTS

Words in the glossary appear in **bold** type the first time they are used in the text.

RAIN, RAIN, GO AWAY!

Rainy days aren't often welcome. They ruin picnics and soccer games, and keep everyone inside. However, rain can bring one of nature's most beautiful light shows—a rainbow! Rainbows are the colored **arcs** that form across the sky when the sun comes out during a rainstorm.

Rainbows occur because of the way sunlight passes through raindrops. In order to learn how sun and rain make a rainbow, it's important to understand prisms. By shining a light into a prism, you can create a rainbow!

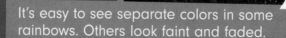

It's easy to see separate colors in some rainbows. Others look faint and faded.

EYE ON THE SKY

Light is made up of waves. Prisms, raindrops, and other **mediums** affect the movement of these waves.

PRISMS

A prism is a piece of glass that's shaped like a triangle and has many **facets**. When light meets one of these facets, it "bends" or changes directions. This is called refraction. Refraction happens because light moves faster through the air than through the prism.

Think of refraction like a shopping cart that's moving across a parking lot when its right front wheel hits a patch of grass. Just as a prism slows and turns light, the grass slows the wheel and causes the cart to turn right.

Shine a light through this prism to create a rainbow!

Light is refracted twice when it passes through a prism—first when it enters the prism and again when it leaves the prism.

Prisms can create many rainbows at once.

LIGHT AND COLOR

The light we can see is called visible light. It's sometimes called white light, but it's not white! It's made up of colors. Refraction causes a beam of light to separate into the colors that form a rainbow. They separate because of the differences in their **frequency** and **wavelength**.

Each color has a different frequency and moves through the prism at a different speed. A color's wavelength affects the **angle** at which it bends when it's refracted. Colors with longer wavelengths, like red, bend less than blue and violet, which have shorter wavelengths.

When a prism separates light into colors we can see, it's called dispersion.

long wavelengths (red) refracted less

white light

prism

short wavelengths (violet) refracted more

This illustration shows how "white" light separates into colors when it enters and leaves a prism.

RAINDROPS

The formation of a rainbow in the sky begins when sunlight enters a raindrop and refracts. However, unlike a prism, the curved inside of the raindrop then **reflects** the light back in the direction it came from. As light exits the raindrop, it's refracted again and the colors spread out.

Many raindrops are needed to make a rainbow. Each drop only supplies one color to the rainbow. This color is the only one that exited the drop at the correct angle for us to see it.

EYE ON THE SKY

Because light reflects inside a raindrop, the sun will always be behind you and the rain in front of you when you look at a rainbow.

white light

sun

water drop

our eye

DOUBLE RAINBOWS

Have you ever seen two rainbows at once? The main rainbow is clearer and has darker colors. The second rainbow appears above the primary rainbow and is fainter.

Secondary rainbows form when light reflects twice within a raindrop. The reflections then exit the raindrop at different angles. The size of the raindrop must be just right for this to occur. Because the secondary rainbow results from a second reflection of light inside the raindrop, its colors are in the opposite order of the primary rainbow's!

These rainbows are mirror images of each other.

It's possible for more than two rainbows to form. However, these "higher order" rainbows are often too faint to be seen.

Seeing a double rainbow like this one can brighten any rainy day!

ROY G. BIV

An easy way to remember the colors of the rainbow is by using a made-up name: Roy G. Biv. Each letter stands for one of the colors in the order we see them in the sky. Did you know there are other colors in a rainbow? We just can't see them as clearly.

A rainbow is called a "bow" because, like a bow on a present, it's made up of a series of arcs that have the same center.

Red
Orange
Yellow
Green
Blue
Indigo
Violet

EYE ON THE SKY

A raindrop creates a circular rainbow. However, the curve of Earth blocks all but an arc.

OTHER NATURAL RAINBOWS

Just like sunlight, bright moonlight can cause a rainbow. **Lunar** rainbows are much fainter than those caused by the sun. Even a full moon's light isn't as strong as sunlight. These special rainbows have been observed for thousands of years, but aren't seen very often.

Have you ever seen a rainbow painted across a cloud? These "fire clouds" cause rainbows because they're full of ice crystals. Light moves through them just like it does through prisms!

Some rainbows aren't shaped like an arc, but they're still beautiful!

No observer can look at a rainbow from the exact same angle as another observer, so everyone sees a slightly different rainbow.

This lunar rainbow was seen over Victoria Falls, a waterfall in Africa.

WHEN TO LOOK

Generally, it must be raining and the sun must be shining in order for a rainbow to form. That means it's more likely for rainbows to be seen in summer than in winter, when rain turns to snow and ice.

The best time to see a rainbow is when the sun is close to the **horizon**. More of the full rainbow circle can be seen then. At sunset, you might be able to see a half circle of rainbow in the sky instead of just an arc.

The top of a rainbow that happens at sunset is very high in the sky.

Sunsets draw attention to the reds in a rainbow.

EYE ON THE SKY

If you try to move toward a rainbow, it will move, too. The raindrops that form the bow are at different places in the sky, so it will always seem like the rainbow is moving away.

19

THE END OF THE RAINBOW

During the 17th century, people in Ireland would say that finding a pot of gold was as possible as finding the end of a rainbow. Even then it was known that we can only see part of a rainbow. There's no end of a rainbow—or pot of gold—to find!

Over time, the Irish saying changed, and people began saying there was a pot of gold at the end of the rainbow! Drawings and cartoons of rainbows often show a pot of gold at the rainbow's end.

HOW DOES A RAINBOW FORM?

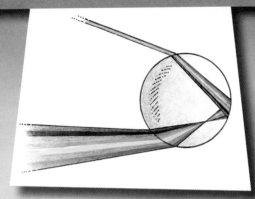

1. The sun comes out while it's raining.

2. Sunlight refracts as it enters a raindrop.

3. The light reflects inside the raindrop.

4. The reflection refracts again as it exits the raindrop.

5. When this occurs in many raindrops, a rainbow appears in the sky.

GLOSSARY

angle: the space between two lines starting from the same point

arc: a curved line

facet: one of the flat surfaces of a prism

frequency: the number of times a wave moves past a point in one second

horizon: the line where Earth's surface seems to meet the sky

lunar: having to do with the moon

medium: the substance in which something lives or acts

reflect: to bounce off something

wavelength: the distance between two peaks in a wave, such as a light wave

FOR MORE INFORMATION

Books

Hartman, Eve, and Wendy Meshbesher. *Light and Sound*. Chicago, IL: Raintree Publishing, 2011.

Orme, Helen. *The Weather: The Best Start in Science*. Mankato, MN: New Forest Press, 2010.

Stewart, Melissa. *Why Do We See Rainbows?* New York, NY: Marshall Cavendish Benchmark, 2009.

Websites

Kids' Crossing: Stuff in the Sky
eo.ucar.edu/kids/sky/colors1.htm
Read more about how rainbows and other weather occurrences happen.

Science Kids
www.cs.dartmouth.edu/farid/Hany_Farid/Science_Kids/Science_Kids.html
Find out the answers to many science questions, including why rainbows form and how airplanes fly.

INDEX